THIS WALKER BOOK BELONGS TO:

_____

For Marianne and Mark
M. H.

To Australian Kath
K. M.

This edition published 2006 for Index Books Ltd
First published 2003 by Walker Books Ltd
87 Vauxhall Walk, London SE11 5HJ

2 4 6 8 10 9 7 5 3 1

Text © 2003 Meredith Hooper
Illustrations © 2003 Katharine McEwen

This book has been typeset in Tempus Sans

Printed in China

British Library Cataloguing in Publication Data:
a catalogue record for this book
is available from the British Library

ISBN 0-7445-8300-4

www.walkerbooks.co.uk

Woolly Jumper
The Story of Wool

MEREDITH HOOPER

illustrated by
KATHARINE MCEWEN

WALKER BOOKS
AND SUBSIDIARIES
LONDON · BOSTON · SYDNEY · AUCKLAND

This is the sheep
That stood in the field
And ate the grass.

This is the farmer
Who owned the sheep
That stood in the field
And ate the grass.

This is the dog
Who mustered the sheep
That stood in the field
And ate the grass.

This is the shearer
Who sheared the sheep
That stood in the field
And ate the grass.

This is the shed-hand
Who picked up the fleece
All springy and soft
That came from the sheep
That stood in the field
And ate the grass.

This is the classer
Who checked the length
And tested the strength
And graded the wool
That came from the sheep
That stood in the field
And ate the grass.

This is the presser
Who took a bale
And pressed it full
Of the very best wool
That came from the sheep
That stood in the field
And ate the grass.

MUNGO
AAAM

106

311313

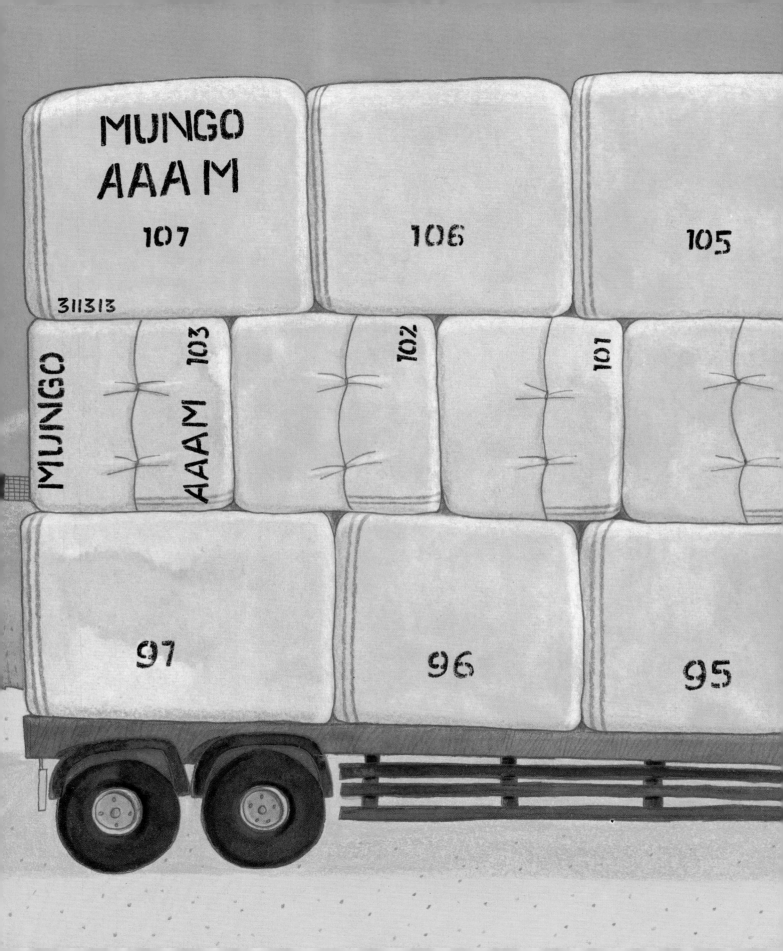

This is the carrier
Who drove his truck
And loaded it up
And carried the wool
That came from the sheep
That stood in the field
And ate the grass.

104

99

86

94

JOE CARRIER & Co.

This is the buyer
Who looked at the wool
And bought the best -
Leaving the rest -
That came from the sheep
That stood in the field
And ate the grass.

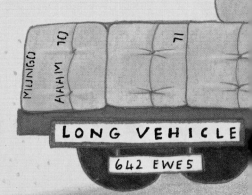

LONG VEHICLE

642 EWES

WIRRA
AAAM

104

WIRRA

This is the mill
That took the wool

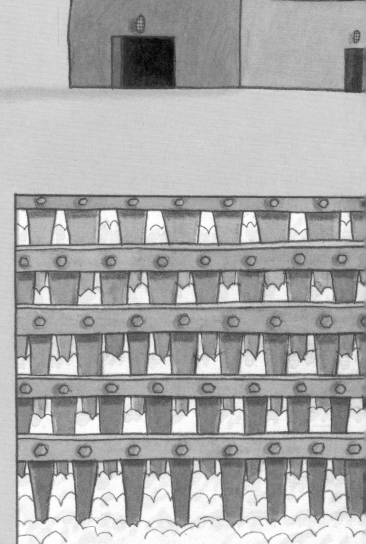

And scoured

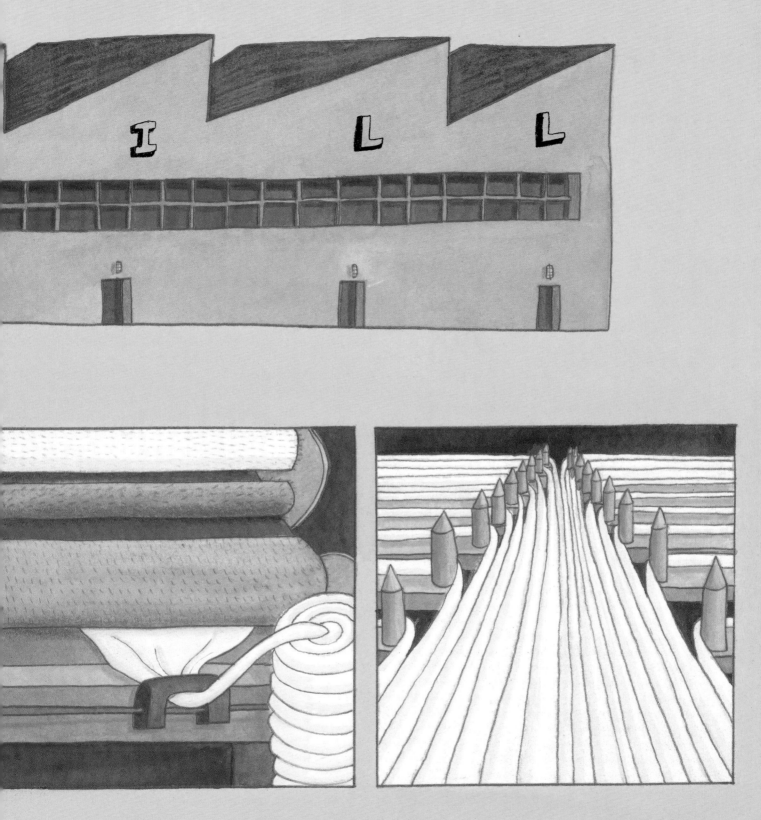

and carded   and combed it

And twisted and spun and dyed it
Winding it up
In bright-coloured balls
Of soft springy wool
That came from the sheep
That stood in the field
And ate the grass.

This is the aunty
Who went to the shop
And bought the balls
Of bright-coloured wool
That came from the sheep
That stood in the field
And ate the grass

And knitted ...

and knitted ...

and knitted ...

and knitted ...

a warm woolly jumper.

And this is Jack
Wearing the jumper
Made of the wool
That came from the sheep
That ate more grass
And grew more wool.

About this book

The sheep in this book live on a big farm in Australia.

The farmer has 6,000 merino sheep. Merino sheep grow beautiful crinkly wool. Sometimes kangaroos jump across the fences into the paddocks where the sheep are eating grass. Kangaroos like eating grass too!

The farmer's dog is called Bella. She is a very good sheepdog. Every spring Bella helps the farmer round up, or "muster" the sheep ready for shearing. The farmer uses a four-wheeled motorbike with big fat tyres.

The sheep are taken to the wool shed. Here the shearers are ready to start work. Shearers can shear 100–200 sheep in a day. The fastest shearer is called "The Gun". The fleece is shorn off in one big piece and falls on the floor in a heap. Shorn sheep look much thinner!

Everyone works hard in the shearing shed. Bella helps too. She can even run across the sheep's backs.

The classer looks at each fleece and grades it. The farmer hopes that his wool will be "AAAM", which means Triple A merino wool - the best.

Then the fleeces are put in the wool press.